THE
POCKET BOOK
OF
FLAGS

Vineyard Books

Project Editor: Fiona Gold
Cartographic Manager: Richard Watts
Designer: Frankie Wood
Proof Reader: Lin Thomas
Production: Clive Sparling

Vineyard Books is an imprint of
Andromeda Oxford Ltd.

Planned and produced by
Andromeda Oxford Ltd
11–15 The Vineyard
Abingdon
Oxfordshire OX14 3PX

ISBN 1-871869-71-4

Origination by Global Colour, Malaysia

Flags produced by Lovell Johns, Oxford, UK,
and authenticated by The Flag Research
Center, Winchester, Mass. 01890, USA,
and by The Flag Institute, 10 Vicarage Road,
Chester CH2 3HZ, England.

Printed by K.H.L. Printing Co. Ltd., Singapore

CONTENTS

THE POLITICAL WORLD

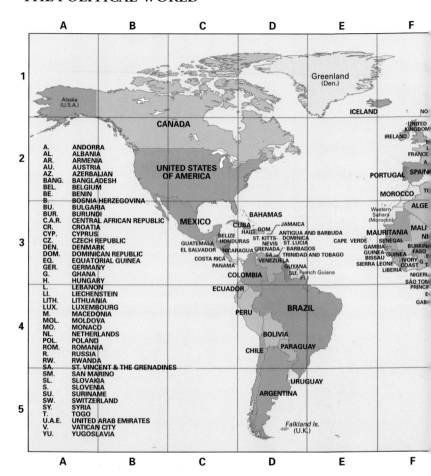

A.	ANDORRA
AL.	ALBANIA
AR.	ARMENIA
AU.	AUSTRIA
AZ.	AZERBAIJAN
BANG.	BANGLADESH
BEL.	BELGIUM
BE.	BENIN
B.	BOSNIA-HERZEGOVINA
BU.	BULGARIA
BUR.	BURUNDI
C.A.R.	CENTRAL AFRICAN REPUBLIC
CR.	CROATIA
CYP.	CYPRUS
CZ.	CZECH REPUBLIC
DEN.	DENMARK
DOM.	DOMINICAN REPUBLIC
EQ.	EQUATORIAL GUINEA
GER.	GERMANY
G.	GHANA
H.	HUNGARY
L.	LEBANON
LI.	LIECHTENSTEIN
LITH.	LITHUANIA
LUX.	LUXEMBOURG
M.	MACEDONIA
MOL.	MOLDOVA
MO.	MONACO
NL.	NETHERLANDS
POL.	POLAND
ROM.	ROMANIA
R.	RUSSIA
RW.	RWANDA
SA.	ST. VINCENT & THE GRENADINES
SM.	SAN MARINO
SL.	SLOVAKIA
S.	SLOVENIA
SU.	SURINAME
SW.	SWITZERLAND
SY.	SYRIA
T.	TOGO
U.A.E.	UNITED ARAB EMIRATES
V.	VATICAN CITY
YU.	YUGOSLAVIA

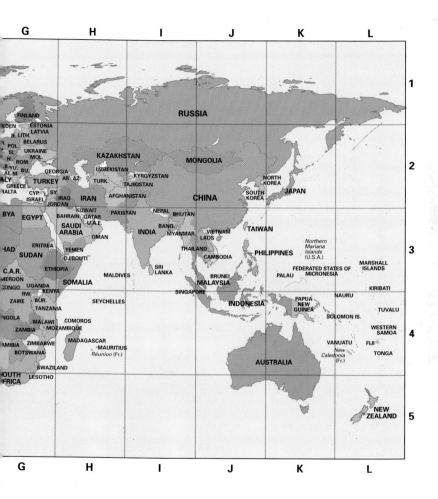

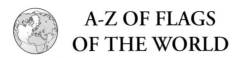

A-Z OF FLAGS
OF THE WORLD

Introduction

Flags have existed for over 3,000 years. The earliest, called vexilloids, were wooden or metal poles topped with a carving. About 2,000 years ago pieces of fabric were added for decoration. Over the next 500 years the free-flying fabric part of the flag became more important than the pole. As heraldry developed in the Middle Ages, noble families created fabric banners showing their coat of arms, and new ground rules were established governing flag design and use. As time moved on, the need for a simple means of identification of ships at sea led to the standardization of national flags.

Today every independent country has a national flag. Some countries may use variations of their national flag for different purposes: governmental or state flags usually incorporate an emblem such as a coat of arms; and there are often special versions of the flag only used at sea, called naval ensigns. Usually there is a religious or political mythology attached to the flag explaining what the colors and emblems mean.

It is quite common for a country to alter its flag in order to incorporate the colors or symbols of a religious or political grouping with which it wants to identify. For example, Communist states often adopt a red flag showing the tools of the industrial and agricultural laborer. The colors and emblems of some of the main groupings are given on page 59; they are referred to in the text with the symbol (▶ page 59).

The following pages show the national flags for each independent country, as well as the state or territory flags of some nations. They are accompanied by a location map showing where the country is, including a grid reference to the world map on pages 4-5.

AFGHANISTAN

Introduced in 1993. The emblem includes elements from earlier versions of the arms, as well as religious inscriptions.

ALBANIA

A double-headed eagle is the national symbol, representing the citizens' name for themselves "people of the eagle". A yellow star was added in 1946 and removed in 1992.

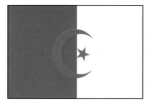

ALGERIA

Originally the flag of the liberation movement, it was adopted as the national flag following independence in 1962. Green represents Islam (▶ page 59), white is for purity and red is for independence.

ANDORRA

Combines the national colors of France and Spain which, historically, administered Andorra jointly. This flag is identical to the Romanian flag except for the coat of arms.

ANGOLA

The half cog wheel and sickle (like the Soviet hammer and sickle) represent industrial and agricultural labor. Red represents the bloodshed of the fight for independence, and black represents Africa.

ANTIGUA AND BARBUDA

Introduced in 1967, the flag reuses the rising sun emblem from the old coat of arms, in a V-shape for victory. Red is for the dynamism of the people, blue for hope, and white for the sea.

ARGENTINA

The blue and white colors were used by the forces for independence against Spain, and were adopted in General Belgrano's design following victory in May 1810. The emblem known as the "Sun of May" was added in 1818.

ARMENIA

The flag was first used in 1918 and was revived in 1990 following the collapse of communism. The design represents a rainbow over Mount Ararat.

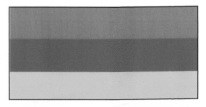

AUSTRALIA

K4

Dating from 1909, the Australian flag features a Union Jack, the "Commonwealth" star and, representing Australia itself, the five stars of the Southern Cross constellation.

States and Territories

The state flags are based on the British Blue Ensign, flown during the colonial period. The state badges are from the national coat of arms, and the Southern Cross emblem represents Australia. The flag of the Northern Territory was adopted in 1978. Black, white and ocher are the official colors of the territory, and the device is a Sturt's desert rose. The Capital Territory flag was introduced in 1993. The white and blue swans represent white and aboriginal citizens, the castle stands for Canberra and the crown represents the monarch.

Australian Capital Territory

New South Wales

Northern Territory

Queensland

South Australia

Tasmania

Victoria

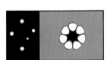

Western Australia

AUSTRIA

The red-white-red flag of Austria dates back to the 12th century, and is one of the oldest in continuous use. In this form it became the national flag in 1918.

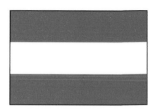

AZERBAIJAN

This is a variation of the flag first used in 1918. It was adopted in this form in 1991 following independence from the former Soviet Union. The crescent and star are Pan-Islamic emblems (▶ page 59).

BAHAMAS

Adopted in 1973, the colors of the Bahamian flag symbolize the aquamarine seas around the islands and the golden sands of the beaches. The black triangle symbolizes the strength of the people.

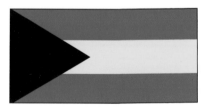

BAHRAIN

As a British colony from 1820, Bahrain was obliged to adopt the British Red Ensign. After independence in 1971, it evolved a red flag showing a white strip with 8 points. Qatar's has 9 points.

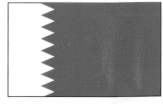

BANGLADESH

Introduced in 1971 when Bangladesh became independent from Pakistan, the red disc ("sun of freedom") originally contained a silhouette of the country, but this was dropped in 1972.

BARBADOS

Adopted following independence in 1966, the "broken" trident of the god of the sea (Neptune) not only represents the island's dependence on the sea but also symbolizes a clean break with the past.

BELARUS

Adopted in 1995 following independence from the former Soviet Union in 1991. Red represents the state's Communist history, green its lush vegetation, and a traditional woven design runs near the hoist.

BELGIUM

Flanders, Brabant and Wallonia used these three colors in their struggle for independence from the Netherlands in 1830. Adopted in the national flag in 1831.

BELIZE

The colors represent the two main political parties after independence in 1981. The coat of arms, surrounded by a green garland, shows the importance of woodcutting to the first colonists.

BENIN

The Pan-African colors (▶ page 59) of this flag were originally adopted following autonomy in 1959, and were reinstated after a period of Communist government 1975–90.

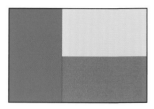

BHUTAN

The wingless dragon, clutching four white gems, is the symbol of Bhutan, the land of the thunder dragon. Yellow represents the temporal power of the king, red the spiritual power of the lamas.

BOLIVIA

In the colors of the flag red represents courage, green is for the fertile land and yellow for rich natural resources. This version, based on the original design of 1825, dates from 1851.

BOSNIA HERZEGOVINA

The flag was adopted by the newly independent republic in 1992. It features the shield of a medieval king of Bosnia.

BOTSWANA

Adopted in 1966, following independence. The blue background stands for the importance of rain to this dry country. The black and white stripes stand for racial harmony.

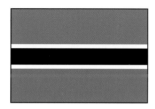

BRAZIL

Green and yellow were the colors of Brazil's hero of independence, Dom Pedro. The blue disc shows the stars over Rio de Janeiro on November 15, 1889. Four new stars were added in 1992, representing four new federal states.

BRUNEI

Originally a plain yellow flag, showing the color of the sultan, the black and white stripes were added in 1906 to represent his chief ministers. The arms were added in 1959.

13

BULGARIA

Dating from 1878, the Bulgarian tricolor is based on the Pan-Slav colors (▶ page 59) with the blue stripe of the Russian tricolor changed to green.

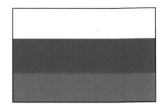

BURKINA FASO

Adopted in 1984, this flag uses the Pan-African colors (▶ page 59) also flown by most of Burkina Faso's neighbors. The central star may vary in size.

BURUNDI

Adopted in 1962, the Burundi flag has retained its original background design. In 1967 the central emblem was altered from a Tutsi drum to three stars that represent the three main ethnic groups.

CAMBODIA

The towers of the famous temple of Angkor Wat have always featured on the flag, but the background has changed often. The current version was adopted in 1993.

CAMEROON

Adopted in 1975, the flag features the Pan-African colors (▶ page 59). Former French colonies often base their flag design on a vertical tricolor. The star represents unity.

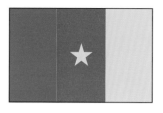

CANADA *see page* 16

CAPE VERDE

Introduced in 1992 and replacing a former flag using Pan-African colors (▶ page 59). The ten stars represent the ten islands of Cape Verde.

CENTRAL AFRICAN REPUBLIC

Adopted in 1958, this flag combines the French tricolor and the Pan-African colors (▶ page 59). While celebrating independence it also expresses a wish to remain politically close to France.

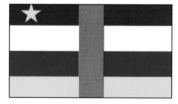

CHAD

This flag was adopted in 1959, the year before independence from France. The design is based on the French tricolor, replacing the white stripe with yellow from the Pan-African colors (▶ page 59).

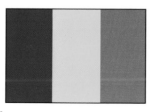

CANADA

The maple leaf design was adopted in 1965. The two red stripes represent the Pacific and Atlantic Oceans.

Provinces and Territories

Ontario and Manitoba have flags based on the Red Ensign, a British naval flag used (with the Canadian shield in the fly) as the official flag of Canada until 1965. Prince Edward Island and New Brunswick both use the lion emblem from the Royal Standard of the United Kingdom, and British Columbia uses the Union Jack with emblems for the sun and sea. Quebec, formerly a French colony, retains the French fleur de lis. Nova Scotia's flag is based on the Scottish cross of St. Andrew. Other states have produced individual designs using local emblems and often incorporating the Canadian colors, red and white.

Alberta

British Columbia

Manitoba

New Brunswick

Newfoundland

Northwest Territories

Nova Scotia

Ontario

Prince Edward Island

Quebec

Saskatchewan

Yukon Territory

CHILE

Inspired by the Stars and Stripes of the United States, this flag dates from 1817. The star is to guide Chile to an honorable future.

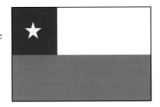

CHINA

Introduced in 1949 and based on the Soviet Red Flag. The large star stands for unity, and the four smaller ones for the social classes: workers, peasants, bourgeoisie and patriotic capitalists.

COLOMBIA

Yellow, blue and red were the colors of the Venezuelan rebel, Francisco Miranda, who tried to liberate New Granada (as it was then) from the Spanish in 1806. The flag was originally adopted in 1819.

COMOROS

This features the Islamic green background and crescent (▶ page 59), and a star for each island. The orientation of the emblems has changed often, this version dates from 1995.

17

CONGO

Introduced in 1959 and used until 1970 when the Communist regime came to power. Reintroduced in 1991. Like many flags in the region it uses the Pan-African colors (▶ page 59).

COSTA RICA

Introduced in 1848, based on the blue and white flag of the United Provinces of Central America. The red stripe was added in honor of revolutionary France. The crest has been modified several times.

CROATIA

This version of the Pan-Slav colors (▶ page 59) was adopted in 1848, and reintroduced following independence in 1991. The central shield, added in 1991, represents areas of land claimed by Croatia.

CUBA

Designed in 1848 in the United States, and used since 1902. The star (La Estrella Solitaria) represented a wish that the state of Cuba would add one more star to the US flag.

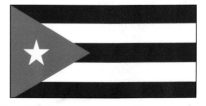

CYPRUS

Adopted in 1960 following independence from Britain. The white background signifies peace, and two olive branches cross below the outline of the island.

CZECH REPUBLIC

After Czechoslovakia split into two states in 1992, the Czech Republic kept the former flag, introduced in 1920, using the Pan-Slav colors (▶ page 59).

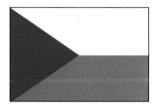

DENMARK

One of the oldest national flags, reputed to have been in continuous use since 1219. It has influenced the designs of the other Scandinavian flags.

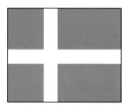

DJIBOUTI

Adopted in 1977 following independence from France. The design and colors are based on the flag of the Djibouti freedom fighters, with the red star for unity.

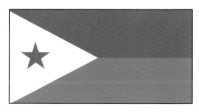

DOMINICA

Dating from 1978, this is the only national flag to feature a parrot. The sisserou, unique to Dominica, has become a national emblem. The surrounding stars represent island parishes.

DOMINICAN REPUBLIC

Created in 1844 by adding a central white cross to the flag of the neighboring country, Haiti, and putting the colors in opposite corners. The coat of arms shows an open Bible.

ECUADOR

Adopted in 1900, some 70 years after Ecuador severed its political connection with Colombia. The colors are the same as the Colombian flag, but with Ecuador's coat of arms in the center.

EGYPT

Dates from 1984, and features the Pan-Arab colors (▶ page 59). The central emblem is the eagle of Saladin, the crest of a famous Muslim ruler.

EL SALVADOR

Introduced in 1972, using the blue and white colors of the former United Provinces of Central America (see Honduras, Guatemala, Nicaragua and Costa Rica). The arms are featured in the center.

EQUATORIAL GUINEA

Adopted on independence in 1968. Green represents natural resources, red the struggle for independence, and white stands for peace. The blue triangle is the sea that links all parts of the state together.

ERITREA

One of the newest national flags, adopted when Eritrea became independent from Ethiopia in 1993. The design is based on the flag of the Eritrean People's Liberation Front.

ESTONIA

Introduced in 1881 and used as the national flag from 1920 until the Soviet flag replaced it in 1924. It was revived in 1991 following independence.

ETHIOPIA

Adopted in 1897 in the colors of the Rastafarian movement. This was one of the two original flags that inspired the Pan-African colors (▶ page 59).

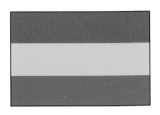

FEDERATED STATES OF MICRONESIA

This form of the flag was adopted in 1978. The stars stand for the states in this group of islands, and the deep blue background represents the Pacific Ocean.

FIJI

Adopted in 1970 following independence, the Union Jack represents Fiji's membership of the British Commonwealth. The coat of arms dates from 1908, and shows a dove of peace.

FINLAND

Dates from 1918 and, like other Scandanavian flags, is based on the design of the Danish flag. The colors represent lakes and snow.

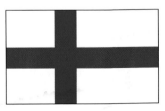

FRANCE

First used in this form in 1794 following the French Revolution. The tricolor has inspired many flag designers in new republics around the world.

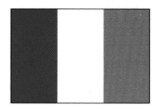

GABON

Adopted in 1960 just before independence from France. The colors represent the forests, the sun and the sea.

GAMBIA

Adopted in 1965 on independence from Britain. The central blue stripe stands for the Gambia river, red for sunshine, green for nature, and white for unity and peace.

GEORGIA

Designed in 1917 and revived in 1990 on the collapse of Communism. The distinctive cherry red background stands for the joyful past and present, black for the period of Soviet rule, and white for hope.

GERMANY

East and West Germany reunited in 1990. They kept the flag first used by the Weimar Republic in 1819, and used by West Germany following World War II.

GHANA

Introduced in 1957. It was the first modern flag using all the Pan-African colors (▶ page 59), and inspired many other flags for neighboring states. The black star is the "lodestar of African Freedom".

GREECE

Dates from 1830 following liberation from the Ottoman Empire. The nine stripes are said to stand for the nine syllables in the Greek motto meaning "Liberty or Death!".

GRENADA

Dates from 1974 and features a stylized nutmeg, the country's main export. Red, yellow and green were used on the flags of all the islands in the West Indies at some time.

GUATEMALA

Adopted in 1839 using the blue and white of the former United Provinces of Central America (see El Salvador, Costa Rica, Honduras, and Nicaragua). Guatemala's national coat of arms is in the center.

GUINEA

Introduced following independence from France in 1958. The design is based on the French tricolor, but using the Pan-African colors (▶ page 59).

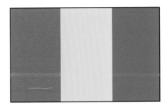

GUINEA-BISSAU

Adopted in 1974 following independence from Portugal. It uses the Pan-African colors (▶ page 59) and the black star of African freedom first used on the flag of Ghana.

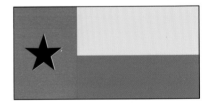

GUYANA

Adopted following independence in 1966, this design in the Pan-African colors (▶ page 59) is known as the "Golden Arrow". It is said to represent the dynamism and zeal of a young country.

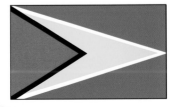

HAITI

Adopted in 1803, this flag alternated and co-existed with a red and black flag. Duvalier used the red and black flag from 1964; this one was reintroduced after the flight of "Baby Doc" Duvalier in 1986.

HONDURAS

Based on the colors of the United Provinces of Central America, the five stars represent the original member countries. (See also El Salvador, Costa Rica, Guatemala and Nicaragua).

HUNGARY

These have been the national colors of Hungary since the 17th century. This version of the flag dates from 1848. In 1949 a Communist symbol was added, and dropped after the 1956 rising.

ICELAND

This version of the Icelandic flag dates from 1913. It is exactly the same design as the Norwegian flag, with the red and blue colors reversed.

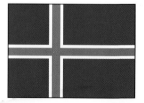

INDIA

Adopted in 1947 just before independence, and based on the flag of the Indian National Congress. The central image is a Buddhist wheel of life dating back 2,000 years.

INDONESIA

Adopted in 1949 when Indonesia became independent of the Netherlands. Red and white are said to be the colors of the medieval empire of Majapahit.

IRAN

Adopted in 1980, using the national colors from the 18th century. The lettering says *Allahu Akbar* ("God is Great") 22 times. The emblem, a sword and crescents, expresses Islamic revolution (▶ page 59).

IRAQ

This dates from 1963, using Pan-Arab colors (▶ page 59). The three stars predicted a union of Iraq, Egypt and Syria. During the Gulf War the words *Allahu Akbar* ("God is Great") were added.

IRELAND

Based on the French tricolor, this design dates from 1848 and became the national flag in 1919. The colors represent green for the nationalists, orange for the Ulster Protestants and white for peace.

ISRAEL

Introduced in 1948 on the formation of the state of Israel. The emblem is the Star of David. White and blue are said to be derived from the colors of the traditional prayer shawl.

ITALY

Adopted in 1848, the Italian tricolor is a direct copy of the French Revolutionary flag, substituting colors used in the Italian flag since 1797.

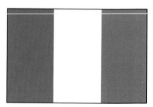

IVORY COAST

Adopted in 1959, a year before independence. It is a tricolor design with orange for the dry northern savanna and green for the southern forests. The colors are in reverse order to those on the Irish flag.

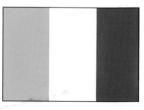

JAMAICA

D3

Designed in 1962, just before independence. The colors stand for hope, natural resources and hardships to be overcome.

JAPAN

K2

Adopted as a marine flag in 1854, the central red disc represents the rising sun referred to in Japan's name *Nihon* "Land of the Rising Sun". The white background represents purity and honesty.

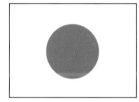

JORDAN

G2

Adopted in 1921, and based on the Pan-Arab colors (▶ page 59). The white star with seven points was added in 1928 to represent the provinces in the region that the Hashemites claimed.

KAZAKHSTAN

H2

Designed in 1992 after the breakup of the Soviet Union. It features the sun and a soaring eagle. There is a traditional Kazakh design on the hoist.

KENYA

Adopted in 1963 and based on the flag of the main political party – the Kenya African National Union. The dark red of the central band is known as "Kenya Red".

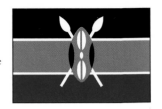

KIRIBATI

Kiribati, formerly the British Protectorate of the Gilbert Islands, gained independence in 1979. The coat of arms granted in 1937 was adapted for the flag.

KUWAIT

Introduced in 1961, when Kuwait became independent of Britain. The tricolor and trapezium design uses the Pan-Arab colors (▶ page 59).

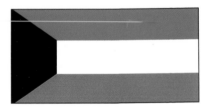

KYRGYSTAN

Originally adopted in 1992 after the collapse of the Soviet Union; this version dates from 1993. The central emblem is a traditional Kyrgyzstani tent.

LAOS

Adopted in 1975 after some years of unofficial use by the Lao Patriotic Front. The white full moon stands for the future.

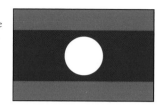

LATVIA

Adopted in 1917, but replaced by the Soviet flag from 1924. It was restored in 1990 after the collapse of communism.

LEBANON

The flag was first hoisted in 1943, based on an earlier design. The tree in the center is the famous cedar of Lebanon, associated with the country since the time of King Solomon.

LESOTHO

Adopted in 1987 replacing the flag used since independence in 1966. White, blue and green represent peace, rain and plenty. The device is a silhouette of the national shield.

31

LIBERIA

F3

Modeled on the US flag following Liberia's colonization by a group of Afro-Americans in the 1840s. The 11 stripes represent the 11 signatories of the new state's declaration of independence.

LIBYA

G3

Introduced in 1977. This is the only international flag that uses a plain color with no national symbols. Green is associated with Islam (▶ page 59).

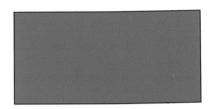

LIECHTENSTEIN

F2

The red and blue colors of Liechtenstein date back to the 19th century. The ducal coronet, representing the ruling family, was added in 1937.

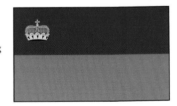

LITHUANIA

G2

First adopted in 1918. It was suppressed during the communist period, when the Soviet flag was used instead, but was restored in 1990 following the collapse of Communism.

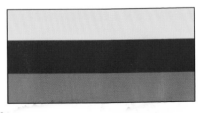

LUXEMBOURG

F2

Red, white and blue have been the national colors of Luxembourg since medieval times. The blue stripe was made paler at the end of the 19th century to distinguish it from the Dutch flag.

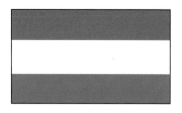

MACEDONIA, former Yugoslav Republic

G2

Originally the flag showed the "Star of Vergina" in the center of a red background, but after disputes with Greece the flag was changed to this one in September 1995.

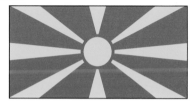

MADAGASCAR

H4

Introduced in 1958 with the formation of the republic. Red and white are the traditional colors of the Merina people, green represents the other main ethnic group, the coastal Hova people.

MALAWI

G4

Adopted on independence in 1964, based on the flag of the Malawi Congress Party. The colors are those of the United Negro Improvement Association (▶ page 59); the rising sun represents a new age.

MALAYSIA

Adopted in 1963, based on the Malay flag. The number of stripes and points on the star rose from 11 to 14 when Singapore, Sabah and Sarawak joined the federation and Malaya became Malaysia.

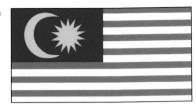

MALDIVES

Adopted in 1965 on independence from Britain. The original flag was red; the addition of the green rectangle and the crescent reflect the importance of Islam (▶ page 59).

MALI

Adopted in 1959, using the Pan-African colors (▶ page 59). Originally the central panel held a black stylized figure of a man, which was dropped in 1961, creating a mirror-image of Guinea's flag.

MALTA

The Maltese flag is in the colors of the Knights of St. John who ruled the island 1530–1802. The medal is the George Cross, awarded to the islanders for bravery during World War II. It was added in 1943.

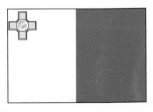

MARSHALL ISLANDS

Dates from 1979 when the islands were under US control. The design was retained after full independence in 1990.

MAURITANIA

Adopted in 1959, the year before Mauritania gained independence from France. The color and symbols express the Islamic foundations of this country (▶ page 59).

MAURITIUS

Adopted following independence from Britain in 1968. The four colors are found in the island's coat of arms, granted in 1906.

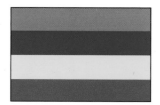

MEXICO

Adopted following independence in 1821, using the colors of the Army of Liberation. The central emblem is the Aztec ideogram for Mexico City, an eagle standing on a cactus while killing a snake.

MOLDOVA

Moldova was once a part of Romania and its flag is based on the Romanian colors with the Moldovan coat of arms in the center.

MONACO

The colors are those of the Grimaldi family who have ruled Monaco since 1297. The flag in this form dates from 1881.

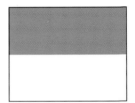

MONGOLIA

Blue, yellow and red are the colors in the arms of Mongolia and have been used in various other combinations on the national flag. The *soyonbo* emblem represents the Buddhist world view.

MOROCCO

Originally this was a plain red flag. The green pentacle, sometimes called Solomon's Seal, was added in 1915.

MOZAMBIQUE

Based on the Pan-African colors (▶ page 59), this flag was introduced in 1983 replacing an earlier design. The emblems are a hoe, a rifle and a book.

MYANMAR

Adopted in 1974 when Burma, as it was then, became a Socialist republic. The emblem is a rice plant inside a cog wheel surrounded by 14 stars, one star for each national state and division.

NAMIBIA

Adopted on independence in 1990, using the colors, but not the design, of the liberation party's flag. The 12 points of the sun may stand for the country's 12 ethnic groups.

NAURU

Adopted on independence in 1968. The flag represents Nauru's geographical position just below the Equator. The 12 points of the star stand for Nauru's 12 ethnic groups.

37

NEPAL

Dating from 1962, this is the only national flag that is not a rectangle. The white shapes represent the sun and moon, and the crimson background is the color of rhododendrons, widespread in the country.

NETHERLANDS

The Dutch tricolor (blue, white and orange) originated circa 1572 with the supporters of William of Orange. The orange band gradually changed to red during the 17th century.

NEW ZEALAND

In 1869, four red stars representing part of the Southern Cross were added to the British Blue Ensign, flown by government ships in colonial New Zealand. This became the official national flag in 1902.

NICARAGUA

Adopted in 1908 and based on the flag of the United Provinces of Central America (see also El Salvador, Costa Rica, Guatemala and Honduras). The Nicaraguan arms are in the center.

NIGER

Adopted in 1959, a year before independence was granted. The disc in the center represents the sun, and the colors represent green for the riverside, white for the savanna and orange for the desert.

NIGERIA

Adopted in 1959, the year before Nigeria achieved full independence from Britain. The design symbolizes a fertile green land divided by the shining Niger river.

NORTH KOREA

Adopted in 1948, using the red, white and blue colors of the former Korean flag. It replaces the *yin-yang* (see South Korea) with the red star, the communist symbol of the Korean Workers' Party.

NORWAY

Dates from 1821, with a few temporary changes in the interim. It became the national flag in 1899. The design is based on the Danish flag with the addition of a blue cross.

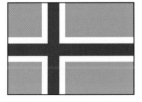

OMAN

Originally a plain red flag. The white and green panels and the emblem of the present dynasty, the Albu Saids, were added in 1970. The emblem is two crossed scimitars and a dagger, linked by a horse bit.

PAKISTAN

Adopted in 1956, based on the 1906 flag of the Muslim League, which led the fight against India for a separate Muslim state. The green background, crescent and star represent Islam (▶ page 59).

PALAU

Adopted following independence in 1994, making it one of the newest of the world's flags. The yellow disk represents a full moon against the blue of the Pacific Ocean.

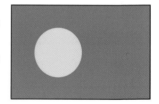

PANAMA

Adopted in 1903 when Panama became independent from Colombia. The colors and design are heavily influenced by the flag of the United States.

PAPUA NEW GUINEA

K4

The flag was designed in 1971. It combines the Southern Cross, representing the former Australian territory of Papua, with the emblem of New Guinea, a bird of paradise.

PARAGUAY

D4

The emblem known as the "Star of May" dates from May 1811 when Spanish rule was overthrown in Paraguay. It was used in a variety of flag designs based on the French tricolor, with this version originating in 1842.

PERU

D4

The red and white colors of the Peruvian Legion were arranged into three vertical stripes by the freedom fighter Simón Bolívar after the defeat of the Spanish in 1824 in Peru and in the territory that became Bolivia.

PHILIPPINES

J3

Designed in 1898 by revolutionaries who wanted to overthrow the Spanish rulers, and adopted in 1946. The nationalist emblems are based on Masonic symbols.

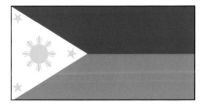

POLAND

Adopted in 1919, using the colors of the Polish arms – a white eagle on a red background in use for several centuries.

PORTUGAL

Adopted in 1911. Green and white were used since the time of the C. 15th king, Henry the Navigator; red is for revolution. The navigator's sphere indicates achievements in world exploration.

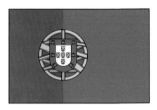

QATAR

Originally white and plain red, based on the flag of Bahrain. Over the years the red has evolved into a shade known as Qatar maroon. The current design was made official in 1949.

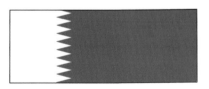

ROMANIA

Adopted in 1867, this combines the colors of the two Ottoman provinces, Wallachia (blue and yellow) and Moldavia (blue and red), that united to form Romania in 1859.

RUSSIA

The Russian tricolor (▶ page 59), was introduced by Peter the Great in 1700 and became the basis for numerous other Slavic flags. It was not used during the Communist period (1917–91).

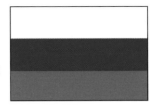

RWANDA

Adopted in 1961 and based on the Pan-African colors (▶ page 59). The letter "R" was added to the central stripe in 1962 to avoid confusion with Guinea's flag.

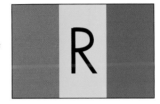

SAINT KITTS-NEVIS

Designed by a local schoolteacher and adopted in 1983 following independence. The colors stand for fertility and freedom, with the two stars representing hope and liberty.

SAINT LUCIA

Adopted in 1967, and representing local mountains, the twin peaks of the Pitons, rising from the sea. The construction of the flag was revised following independence in 1979.

SAINT VINCENT & THE GRENADINES

Introduced in 1985 from a design by a Swiss artist, using colors from the coat of arms on the colonial ensign. The diamonds make a V for Vincent.

SAN MARINO

San Marino is the smallest republic in the world. The colors of the flag are taken from the coat of arms. The design has existed in this form since 1797.

SÃO TOMÉ AND PRÍNCIPE

Introduced on independence in 1975, and based on the Pan-African colors (▶ page 59) following the example set by Ghana.

SAUDI ARABIA

Used in various forms since the 19th century. The Islamic creed appears against a green background (▶ page 59). It reads: "There is no God but Allah, and Muhammad is the Prophet of Allah".

SENEGAL

Senegal shares its flag history with Mali, up to Senegal's secession in 1960, when it kept the Mali flag in Pan-African colors (▶ page 59), but added a green star to differentiate the two.

SEYCHELLES

Adopted in 1977 to replace the flag introduced on independence in 1976. It is based on the flag of the main political party, and represents dawn over the sea.

SIERRA LEONE

Adopted on independence in 1961. This was the winning design in a competition, and uses the main colors from the national coat of arms.

SINGAPORE

Adopted in 1959, and using the white on red crescent and five stars from the coat of arms granted in 1948. The five stars stand for five national ideals: democracy, peace, progress, justice and equality.

SLOVAKIA

First used in 1848, and based on the Pan-Slavic colors (▶ page 59). The Slovakian coat of arms is in the center. It was replaced by the Czecho-slovakian flag 1920–90, and revived after partition.

SLOVENIA

First used (without the coat of arms) in 1848, and based on the Pan-Slavic colors (▶ page 59). The coat of arms dates from the Communist era.

SOLOMON ISLANDS

Adopted in 1978 following independence. The stars represent the original five districts of the country, not the Southern Cross. The yellow band represents sunshine across the green land and blue sea.

SOMALIA

Adopted in 1960 following independence. The colors are from the United Nations flag as Somalia was a former UN territory. The five-pointed star refers to the original five divisions of Somaliland.

SOUTH AFRICA

Adopted on 27 April 1994, marking the end of white minority rule in South Africa. It combines the ANC colors with the major colors in South African flags since 1652.

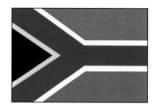

SOUTH KOREA

Adopted in 1950, based on the 1910 pre-Japanese occupation flag. The central *yin-yang* represents the reconciliation of opposites. Around it are the *I-Ching,* the four polarities, against white for peace.

SPAIN

This version dates from 1785, using the traditional red and yellow colors of Aragon and Castile. For official occasions the flag has the Spanish coat of arms near the hoist.

SRI LANKA

Adopted in 1951, when green and orange panels were added to the 1948 flag. The lion, from the coat of arms, is surrounded by four leaves from the bo tree, under which Buddha received enlightenment.

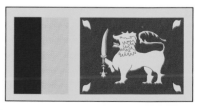

SUDAN

Adopted in 1970, and using the Pan-Arab colors (▶ page 59) popularized by President Nasser of Egypt. This replaced the original flag of independence dating from 1956.

SURINAME

Adopted in 1975 after independence. It combines the colors of the principal political parties at the time. The yellow star, also featured on the coat of arms, stands for unity and hope for the future.

SWAZILAND

Adopted in 1967, the year before independence, and based on the flag of the Swazi Pioneer Corps from World War I. The central shield is of the Emasotsha Regiment, with two spears and a stick behind it.

SWEDEN

The Scandinavian cross (first used by Denmark) dates from 1523, revised in this form in 1906. The colors are taken from the arms of Sweden, three gold crowns on a blue ground.

SWITZERLAND

The white cross on a red background is the badge of the Swiss cantons, adopted by Swiss soldiers in 1339 and made their official banner in 1480. This form dates from 1814; it became the national flag in 1848.

SYRIA

Originally the flag of the United Arab Republic, which Syria joined in 1958. This design was particularly influential in establishing the Pan-Arab colors (▶ page 59). Syria readopted the flag in 1980.

TAIWAN

Known as "white sun in blue sky over red land" this was adopted as the flag of the Republic of China in 1928. When mainland China became a Communist state in 1949, Taiwan retained the former flag.

TAJIKISTAN

Adopted in 1993 following the breakup of the Soviet Union. Tajikistan has ethnic links with Iran and the flags use the same colors.

TANZANIA

Adopted in 1964 when Tanganyika and Zanzibar united to form Tanzania. It combines the colors of the component states so as to give them equal weight.

THAILAND

Adopted in 1917, when a blue stripe was added to the red and white Thai flag to show support for the Allies in World War I, most of whom had red, white and blue flags.

TOGO

Adopted in 1960 just before independence. It is based on the Pan-African colors (▶ page 59) but, unusually, has a white star for national independence rather than a black one.

TONGA

The cross, representing the people's devotion to Christianity, has featured on the Tongan flag since the first one was flown in 1850. This version, designed by a British cleric, dates from 1864.

TRINIDAD AND TOBAGO

Adopted following independence from Britain in 1962. The colors represent vitality (red), purity (white) and the strength of the people (black).

TUNISIA

Based on the flag of the Ottoman Empire (see Turkey), the Tunisian flag dates from about 1835. The crescent and star are traditional Islamic symbols (▶ page 59).

TURKEY

Derived from the flag of the Ottoman empire which introduced the crescent and star emblems in 1801. This version dates from 1936, and has inspired flags of other Islamic states (▶ page 59).

TURKMENISTAN

Introduced in 1992. The design in the hoist is a carpet, the most famous local product. The background is Islamic green with the traditional crescent motif (▶ page 59).

TUVALU

Adopted in 1995. The stars represent the eight inhabited islands that give the state its name *Tuvalu* "eight together". The coat of arms depicts the sea, a traditional meetinghouse, seashells and banana leaves.

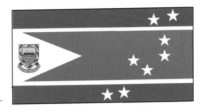

UGANDA

Adopted in 1962, the year before independence, using the colors of the ruling Congress Party. The national symbol, a crested crane, is in the center.

UKRAINE

Dates from 1848. It was used until 1920 but was replaced by the Soviet flag during the period of Communist rule. It was reinstated following independence in 1991.

UNITED ARAB EMIRATES

Introduced in 1971 when the seven emirates were united. In common with many other countries in the region it uses the Pan-Arab colors (▶ page 59).

UNITED KINGDOM

The Union flag is a combination of the crosses of St. George, (England) St. Andrew (Scotland), and St. Patrick (Ireland), This version dates from 1801. A Welsh element is not included in the flag.

Countries of the Union

The English flag, the red cross of St. George on a white background, was first documented in 1277, and has been used continuously since then. The national flag of Scotland, known as the Saltire, is a white diagonal cross on a blue background. It was first documented as the cross of St. Andrew circa 1286–92. The Welsh flag shows the ancient national emblem, a red dragon, on the Tudor colors of the Welsh-born king, Henry VII. The flag of Northern Ireland shows the Red Hand of Ulster from Irish legend, superimposed on the cross of St. George. It was in official use only while there was a government of Northern Ireland (1953–72). More recently it has been adopted by Ulster paramilitaries.

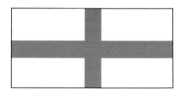

England

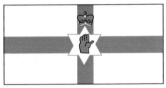

Northern Ireland

Scotland

Wales

UNITED STATES OF AMERICA

C2

Popularly known as the *Stars and Stripes,* the *Star-Spangled Banner,* or *Old Glory,* the 50 stars of the United States' flag stand for the 50 states of the Union, and the 13 stripes for the original 13 states.

The States of the Union

The vast majority of state flags show the badge or emblem of the state against a plain background. A few southern states (Mississippi, Georgia, Alabama and others) incorporate the old Southern Cross from the Civil War period. The national colors are dominant.

Alabama

Alaska

Arizona

Arkansas

California

Colorado

Connecticut

Delaware

Florida

Georgia

Hawaii

Idaho

Illinois

Indiana

Iowa

Kansas

Kentucky

Louisiana

Maine

Maryland

Massachusetts

Michigan

Minnesota

Mississippi

Missouri

Montana

Nebraska

Nevada

New Hampshire

New Jersey

New Mexico

New York

North Carolina

North Dakota

Ohio

Oklahoma

Oregon

Pennsylvania

Rhode Island

South Carolina

South Dakota

Tennessee

Texas

Utah

Vermont

Virginia

Washington

West Virginia

Wisconsin

Wyoming

URUGUAY

Dates from 1830, using the colors and emblem of the Argentinian flag and a design based on the US Stars and Stripes. The nine stripes represent the nine original provinces.

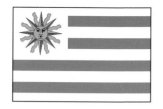

UZBEKISTAN

Dates from 1991 following independence from the former Soviet Union. The moon stands for rebirth and the stars for the importance of astrology and astronomy.

VANUATU

Dates from 1980, using the colors of the main political party. The "Y" represents the layout of the islands of Vanuatu. In the triangle is a boar's tusk, for prosperity, and two crossed fern leaves.

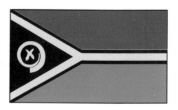

VATICAN CITY

Adopted in 1929. The gold and silver keys of St. Peter, below the papal crown, are used as the emblem. The Vatican colors of yellow and white were adopted in 1808.

VENEZUELA

Dates from 1859, using the colors of the rebel leader Francisco Miranda who fought the Spanish from 1806. The stars represent the original provinces that won independence in 1811.

VIETNAM

Adopted in a slightly different form in 1945, and used by North Vietnam during the civil war. In 1975, following reunification, it was readopted for the whole country.

WESTERN SAMOA

Dates from 1949 when an extra star was added to this stylized representation of the Southern Cross to make it resemble the version on the Australian flag.

YEMEN

Introduced when North and South Yemen were united in 1990. It combines elements from the flags of both former states and uses the Pan-Arab colors (▶ page 59).

YUGOSLAVIA, Serbia/Montenegro

This version of the Pan-Slav colors (▶ page 59) was adopted in 1918 by the former state of Yugoslavia. It continues to be used by the rump state, formed in 1992.

ZAIRE

Introduced in 1971, based on the flag of the main political party and using the Pan-African colors (▶ page 59). It is the third version since independence in 1960. The torch represents the fight for freedom.

ZAMBIA

Adopted in 1964 and based on the colors of the ruling party after independence. The orange stripe represents mineral wealth. The eagle is from the arms of Northern Rhodesia, the state's old colonial name.

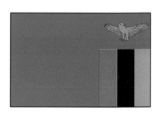

ZIMBABWE

Introduced in 1980, using the Pan-African colors (▶ page 59). The national emblem, a "lightning bird", also known as the Zimbabwe bird, is shown against a red star.

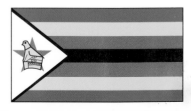

SEMINAL FLAGS

There are several main political or religious groupings of countries that identify themselves by using the same colors in their flags, sometimes even the same emblems, and arranging them in different designs. Here are four of the largest groupings.

PAN-AFRICAN COLORS

The colors (black, red, green and yellow) are derived from two sources: the black, red and green flag of the United Negro Improvement Association created by Marcus Garvey in 1917; and the Ethiopian flag in the Rastafarian colors of green, yellow and red.

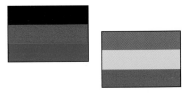

PAN-ARAB COLORS

The colors (black, white, green and red) were used by the Young Arab Society in 1914 and by Sherif Husein of Mecca in 1917. When Husein's son became king of Iraq he adopted the colors in the new flag; other Arab nations followed suit.

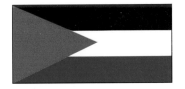

PAN-SLAV COLORS

The Russian tricolor was instituted by Peter the Great in 1700. During the 18th century a Pan-Slav movement gathered force among the Czechs, Slavs and Croats. During 1835–48, as the Austrian empire broke up, emerging Slav states adopted the tricolor in various forms.

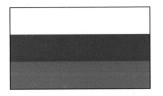

ISLAMIC COLORS

The crescent and star became an emblem of the Ottoman empire from 1793. Abdul Hamid (1876–1909) started a Pan-Islamic movement popularizing the emblem as the international badge of Islam, particularly on a background of green, the color of the Prophet.

FLAGS OF WORLD ORGANIZATIONS

RED CROSS & RED CRESCENT

The Red Cross and Red Crescent flags are used by international medical aid workers. The Red Cross, the Swiss flag in reverse, dates from 1863. The Red Crescent was adopted in 1906 for use by aid organizations from Islamic countries.

COMMONWEALTH OF INDEPENDENT STATES

Introduced in 1991 following the breakup of the Soviet Union. The design is intended to express unity and harmony, suggesting a developing tree or a bowl preserving light and warmth. The blue background represents peace and spirituality, white is for peace and purity, and gold is for light and lasting values.

EUROPEAN UNION

This is based on the Council of Europe flag, first flown in 1953 showing 15 gold stars (the original number of members) in a circle on a dark blue background. As the number of members changed it was decided to have a fixed number of 12 stars. In this form it became the flag of the European Community, which was renamed the European Union in 1993.

LEAGUE OF ARAB STATES

Based on the original flag of the Arab League formed in 1945. The name of the organization appears in Arabic script in the center, surrounded by a crescent and an intertwined chain, signifying close bonds and solidarity between the member states. The olive branches symbolize peace, and the green background is associated with Islam (◀ page 59).

NORTH ATLANTIC TREATY ORGANIZATION

Member countries of the North Atlantic Treaty Organization (NATO) joined together to protect each other. The blue of their flag represents the Atlantic Ocean and the compass symbol in the middle represents membership from all over the world.

ORGANIZATION OF AFRICAN UNITY

The flag of the Organization of African Unity symbolizes the wish for unity and harmony among African states. The central emblem is a stylized map of Africa set inside a wreath of laurel, symbolizing peace.

SOUTH PACIFIC FORUM

The South Pacific Forum was established in 1971 to promote cooperation among the island states of the region. The flag represents a coral atoll in the blue ocean, and the stars represent the number of member countries.

UNITED NATIONS

The United Nations (UN) promotes world peace and international cooperation. Its flag dates from 1947, and shows the globe flanked by two olive branches. The background is a particular shade known as United Nations blue, also used for the helmets of UN troops to distinguish them from other forces.

DEPENDENCIES, COLONIES AND TERRITORIES

Dependencies, colonies and territories often fly a flag that identifies them with the ruling power by reproducing or adapting the mother nation's flag as part of their own. Most of the UK dependencies shown below have added local badges to the British Blue Ensign, a plain blue flag with the Union Jack in the top left hand quarter, originally used by government ships. Most of the US dependencies have adapted the red, white and blue colors, combining them with the American Eagle, or with variations on the Stars and Stripes. Wallis Island has incorporated the French tricolor, and the Faroe Islands has reversed the red and white of the Danish flag, adding an outline of blue around the Danish cross. The Southern Cross constellation from the Australian flag appears on the Christmas Islands flag. Other dependencies have used more individual symbols including the Norfolk pine (Norfolk Island), a stylized coral atoll (Tokelau) and the three legs of Man (Isle of Man).

American Samoa
(US)

Anguilla
(UK)

Aruba
(Netherlands)

Bermuda
(UK)

British Indian Ocean Territory
(UK)

British Virgin Islands
(UK)

Cayman Islands
(UK)

Christmas Island
(Australia)

Cook Islands
(New Zealand)

Falkland Islands
(UK)

Faroe Islands
(Denmark)

French Polynesia
(France)

Gibraltar
(UK)

Greenland
(Denmark)

Guam
(US)

Guernsey
(UK)

Hong Kong
(UK)

Isle of Man
(UK)

Jersey
(UK)

Montserrat
(UK)

Netherlands Antilles
(Netherlands)

Niue
(New Zealand)

Norfolk Island
(Australia)

Northern Marianas
(US)

Pitcairn Islands
(UK)

Puerto Rico
(US)

Tokelau
(New Zealand)

Turks and Caicos Islands
(UK)

Virgin Islands
(US)

Wallis Island
(France)

INDEX